For the Love of Lolly

The BACKstory of REDBONE'S Famous FRONTman

By Stephen Rosario Pisani

As told to his sister Lisa Brandi

DEDICATION

I dedicate this collection of remembrances to myself.

You heard me right: I dedicate this work to me!

Before Lolly Vegas came into my life, I was spiritually and emotionally unformed like the pods in the film *Invasion of the Body Snatchers*. I looked good; I lived my dream as a musician; I had all the toys a successful lifestyle can bring, from DeLoreans to drones.

I had wine, women, and song, but I was lacking in wisdom and empathy for my fellow man (and woman). I had no clue as to what was important, what would save me, who I could save.

It was Lolly's unconditional love, friendship, and life lessons that woke me from my coma of complacency, and pointed out with a gentle hand that I tended to take more than I gave.

He opened my eyes, my heart, and my horizons.

He connected me to nature and neutralized my negativity. His guidance sparked sensitivity and soul searching, which strengthened every one of my relationships, including the one with myself.

He infused me with his Native American spirit, based on calm and common sense, and helped me wrangle my demons of depression. Because of Lolly, my music had more depth, and I began to take better care of my health.

So why am I dedicating this literary work to myself when it was Lolly's words that forever changed my life?

Because I'm the one that had the fucking brains to listen to him!

CONTENTS

PROLOGUE

"And so I did!"

Stephen Rosario Pisani

"WON'T YOU BE, WON'T YOU BE, PLEASE WON'T YOU BE MY NEIGHBOR?"

Music has been the one consistent presence in my life.

Music has broken my heart, nourished my soul, and put food on my table.

I love it in every form, from A to Z as in from America to Zappa. I have played in bands since I was a young teen – all kinds of bands from rock 'n roll to rhythm and soul.

For several years, I played in a heavy metal band on the weekend and as part of a folk/pop duo during the week. Saturdays were reserved for spandex, eye liner, and Twisted Sister, and Tuesdays belonged to bell-bottom jeans, fringe vests, and "Sister Golden Hair." I performed up and down the East Coast, but I always knew that I wanted to be in California... so after decades of paying tribute to Bread, Bowie, Bon Jovi, and the Backstreet Boys, I finally made the move to Los Angeles to promote my own songs.

Now, of course, everyone aspires to live in the Hollywood Hills, or Beverly Hills, or Malibu. Those neighborhoods are the crème de la crème in terms of real estate, but let's get real… a struggling musician cannot afford those zip codes. Fortunately, we have a location back-up plan: a sort of "Los Angeles Lite" known as The Valley. And that is where I landed.

The name of this star-studded-adjacent hamlet was Encino.

It was the apartment version of the Monkees' song "Pleasant Valley Sunday:"

"Charcoal burning everywhere
Rows of condos that are all the same
And no one seems to care"

But it was affordable, even though the town's lack of style and sophistication made me long to "Take the Last Train to Clarksville!"

As I stated earlier, I lived the life of an East Coast musician.

Let me paint that picture for you. I'd sleep all day, drag my ass out of bed, open an empty fridge, shower, set up my equipment, play four sets, break down my equipment, go to a diner, then home, where I'd sleep all day!

But this was California, the home of morning people who surf, jog, do yoga, and get on my last nerve.

As far as neighbors go, well... that meant nothing to me.

With my lifestyle, I could have shared common walls with Jack the Ripper and Jeffrey Dahmer; our paths would never have crossed because I slept all day and was up all night. In fact, the only neighbor I might have been able to hit up for a cup of sugar would be Count Dracula, since we kept the same hours, but all that was about to change.

I first caught sight of my new neighbor when I got home at the crack of dawn after playing some seedy speakeasy in Reseda (a suburb that made Encino look like Monte Carlo), but hey... a gig's a gig.

I fumbled for my keys in that light that straddles the

dawn. I saw a disheveled figure standing outside his front door smoking. I couldn't tell if he had been up all night or had just stumbled out of bed to indulge his habit.

I nodded, that sort of half-hearted nod that says, "Please don't talk to me," but you want to be polite in case he's a serial killer.

I started to ascend the concrete steps that led to my second floor flat. He looked up, and complimented the shabby patio set on my tiny 2x4 balcony.

I found it odd, because the set was there when I moved in. I was convinced it was left behind because the former tenants feared the wrath of their new neighbor if they had the nerve to pollute the curb with this decrepit table and chairs.

But hey, my new neighbor liked it and he wasn't wielding a knife, so I smiled and said "Goodnight," while fantasizing about a way to have him take it off my hands without letting him in my apartment where he might murder me on the way out.

As I slid the chain across my door, I remember asking myself why he looked so familiar to me.

Now, in a town as crazy and cool as Hollyweird, just about *anyone* could live next door… for California is home to movers and shakers, Dodgers and Lakers, and gold-record makers.

So buckle up, because here's where my story begins...

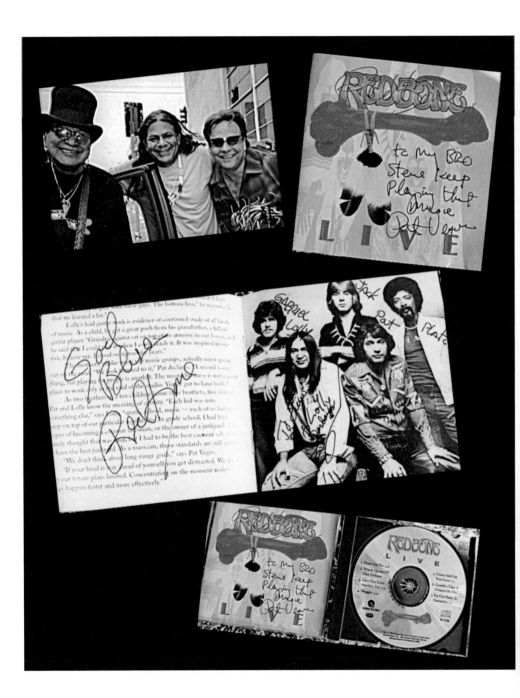

A FRIEND WHO WAS FINE, AND WAS MINE, AND HE MADE MY LIFE DIVINE!

I come from a show biz family.

My mom dated Robert Preston, Tony Bennett, and was engaged to Cliff Robertson.

My Aunt Gloria dated Frank Sinatra and was engaged to Vic Damone.

When my mom and aunts sang at the famed Sands Hotel in Vegas, Jackie Gleason babysat for me and my sisters.

My father, who was an actor, addressed William Friedkin as "Billy Boy," and Steven Spielberg actively fought to cast my uncle Murray Hamilton in his breakout film *Jaws*.

So when I learned that Lolly Vegas (the lead singer of the 70's band Redbone) lived next door, I wasn't exactly starstruck. I liked the band, but they weren't the Stones. Although everyone on this planet knows their mercurial hit song, "Come and Get Your Love," you'd be hard pressed to find many or any people that know the band members by their first names.

Star-struck, no. Lolly-struck... yes!

To me, even though Lolly was a brilliant musician and singer and wrote one of the catchiest rock anthems in modern history, those were by-products of the true talent this man possessed.

He took me under his wing musically, spiritually, and emotionally. I have always suffered from a very vicious strain of depression. It tainted every aspect of my life and plotted against my peace of mind and quest for happiness for as long as I can remember.

Lolly taught me how to face this formidable foe rather than hide from it. He had healing powers for the soul that were passed down from his tribal ancestors and he had tools for coping that I was never able to implement through therapy.

Lolly was a priest, a rabbi, a guru, a medicine man, a mensch, a mentor, and my best friend.

So how did Lolly and I form this everlasting bond?

Well, there was no way to avoid him!

I had to walk past his apartment a dozen times a day to walk my dog, go to the pool, the laundry room, the mailbox, and the garage. Lolly never closed his front door and was an armchair general who would shout things out as I walked by. Soon it became habit that I would just automatically stop at his threshold and say "hi," and then "hi" turned into discussing our musical backgrounds, which turned into sharing war stories from the road, which then became jam sessions, and then breaking bread, and then breaking balls.

With every visit he left me with a word, a thought, an idea, to contemplate and marinate in my brain. I began to see life through a lens of hope and humility.

Lolly was funny and unfiltered in every way.

He was both the most reverent and irreverent person I have ever known.

I think the greatest lesson he ever taught me was that my life was an ongoing work in progress, and how could I possibly judge myself negatively before the work was complete?

He imparted the idea that, like an artist, my only job was to mix my paint with equal parts of self-worth and gratitude, and always use a brush of kindness and love for my fellow man.

Plus he taught me how to make fajitas!

Fate is a strange and glorious thing. If Lolly's apartment was on my left instead of my right, we might have only exchanged a one-time polite nod instead of him becoming one of the most influential people in my life.

Lolly is gone, but my memories are alive and well, and I feel honored and privileged to share the BACKstory of Redbone's FRONTman!

REIGNING CATS AND DOGS

As many of you may or may not know, Native Americans place great value on their heritage and lessons learned from their ancestors. The older the tribe member, the more they are revered and respected by the youngest members of that tribe.

Lolly was a big television addict, and he took great umbrage when nearly every commercial depicted a child being embarrassed by their parent or disrespecting elderly persons by making them seem stupid and feeble.

The Native American culture not only held elders in high esteem, but also placed great reverence on the animal kingdom. Native Americans believe we are one with the earth and even look upon animals as their brothers and sisters. Now, there is probably no greater animal lover than me, but I can honestly say, I never looked at my pets, which I adored, quite like that.

But then, I learned so many valuable life lessons from Lolly.

I have had Great Danes all my life. When it comes to pets, for me, it was the bigger the better, and through the years, when my beloved Danes passed away from old age, they took a piece of my heart and I was never the same.

When I met Lolly, I had a magnificent harlequin Great Dane named Quincy. This majestic black and white canine brought a joy into my life that was, and still is, indescribable. He went everywhere with me. And when I could not take him with me, he waited lovingly by the door until I came home, and greeted me every single time as if I had been away for months, even when I had been away for two minutes to get my mail.

When I moved to my apartment in Encino, California, I never dreamed my next door neighbor would be the front man of the renowned and iconic band Redbone. But Lolly Vegas was indeed the person I would be borrowing a cup of sugar from.

Now when most people walked into Lolly's apartment, their eyes lasered in on the show biz memorabilia, the celebrity photos, the wall of instruments, or the Native American artifacts, but as I shook hands with Lolly for the first time, I locked eyes with a cat.

A jet black feline with turned-up vivid green eyes. This animal could have been Samantha from the TV show *Bewitched* on the many occasions she turned herself into a kitty. He looked part cat, part human and part, well, bewitched!

His name was Asa. Lolly named his beloved pet after his favorite soap opera character from *One Life to Live*. But this cat seemed to have more than one life to live, because he did live to the ripe old age of sixteen.

After taking a moment to admire the unusual beauty of this feline, and feeling the instant and potent chemistry I felt for Lolly, my heart sank. I knew I could never bring my miniature pony of a dog over to visit with Lolly, because Asa clearly ruled the roost. I wasn't worried about Quincy frightening Asa, because as I peered into that cat's supernatural-looking emerald eyes, I was sure Quincy would run for cover the moment he entered Lolly's humble abode.

Lolly and I hit it off immediately. Yes, we had a lot in common: he was a musician, I was a musician; we loved the same foods, the same bands, the same movies; we shared political views as well as world views, plus we were neighbors, but it was much more than that. There was, as the Italians would say, a "simpatico" between us; we were kindred spirits and we quickly became like brothers.

Soon after our first meeting, I invited Lolly to my apartment. Now, when most people walk into my apartment their eyes laser in on the show biz memorabilia, the celebrity photos, the wall of instruments, and my *Italian* artifacts, but Lolly's eyes were transfixed on Quincy who was sitting in the corner like a statue of an Egyptian dog that would have belonged to Pharaoh.

As Lolly shut the door behind him, Quincy immediately ran over to him, slipping on the hardwood floor, wagging his tail, flailing his head back and forth into Lolly's chest, nearly knocking him down while pawing his hand in an effort to be petted. Lolly touched the side of Quincy's massive jaw and just stared into his eyes.

As I witnessed this silent communication between them, I watched my dog transform from a big, clumsy, lovable giant to a serene, enlightened creature that was connected to Lolly—connected to the spirit that Lolly not only saw in him, but respected about him. To this day it gives me chills to remember that moment.

Lolly broke his gaze with my Quincy and turned to me and said, "You must bring Quincy over to meet Asa."

My heart liquefied in my chest as I grabbed Lolly's arm to stop him from walking out the door.

"No, no, no, Lolly, I don't think that's a good idea. What if they get spooked? What if they attack one another, what if..."

At that moment Lolly placed his hand over mine. He looked over at Quincy and in a very soft and soothing voice he said, "Quincy and Asa share the same spirit, and soon they will become brothers, just as you and I have." I released his arm, I released my fear, and Lolly walked out the door. I followed him and Quincy followed me.

Quincy stood by my side in Lolly's doorway as I stroked the top of his head. Without hesitation, Asa strode, almost in slow motion, toward me and Quincy. My instinct was to clutch Quincy's collar, so I could pull him back in case he leapt toward Asa, or in case Asa, with those witchy eyes, leapt toward Quincy.

As Asa got closer, my eyes moved toward Lolly as he sat smiling in his beat-up recliner. Lolly, reassuringly, nodded his head, and I unclenched my grip on Quincy's collar and he sheepishly began to walk toward the very sure-footed Asa.

They met in the middle of the living room. Asa arched his neck to look up at Quincy, who stood a foot taller than him, and then Asa crouched down and began to lick his paws. Quincy took his cue and lay down, resting his oversized snout on the carpet, completely entranced by the primping ritual of the mellow and totally unfazed Asa.

Lolly asked me to grab him something to drink from the fridge, then imitating Dustin Hoffman's character in *Rain Man*, Lolly turned to me and said, "Ten minutes to Wapner." I laughed out loud and handed him a Snapple and the clicker. Lolly watched *The People's Court* and I watched Quincy and Asa basking in the sunlight that streamed thru the plantation shutters.

From that day, Lolly would always call Quincy "mi hijo," which means "my son."

Fast forward...

After Lolly passed away, an assortment of relatives stayed at his home to get his affairs in order. After a day and night of no activity at Lolly's place, I could not help but wonder which family member inherited the precious pet of my dearest pal Lolly. I called one of the relatives and inquired as to Asa's whereabouts.

I was regaled with a laundry list of why no one could take the orphaned Asa. I heard everything from people being allergic, to already having pets, to landlords not allowing animals... but what I didn't hear was where Asa was.

After an awkward silence, I was told that Asa was taken to a nearby animal shelter.

In other words: the pound.

I was very familiar with this hellhole. I knew many people who had rescued dogs and cats from a death sentence there. This place was like Riker's Island for strays, runaways, and discarded animals.

I could feel the veins in my neck becoming engorged with anger as the tears welled up in my eyes. I started to compose a scathing, earth-scorching tirade of words in my head, but as they trickled down to my mouth, only four words came out:

"BRING HIM BACK... NOW!"

I must have put the fear of God into the person on the other end of the phone, because the response was quick and only three words: "I'm leaving now."

Within the hour I was pouring milk into my favorite cereal bowl as those beautiful *Bell, Book and Candle*-like green eyes stared back at me. Quincy lay inches away on his back with his tail beating the floor like a metronome.

I was blessed to have two more years with Asa. He and Quincy became inseparable.

After all, like Lolly said, they were "brothers!"

FOR THE LOVE OF LOLLY

PIANO MAN

Most guitar players look upon their guitars like their children. They very rarely part with them, it's hard to say which one they love more, and though they feel a thrill from buying the latest and greatest model, they will always line up the shiny showstoppers right next to the weathered and worn axes that have served them so well through the years.

Willie Nelson, who can afford any and every guitar ever made, still performs his concerts with a beat-up battered six-string that sports a large hole, and I mean *in addition* to the hole that's supposed to be there.

I guess guitars are like gun belts—the more notches the better! I still have all of my guitars, and I have been playing since the seventies. I love them all equally!

One of the most precious highlights of my time with Lolly Vegas was writing songs together. I would jam on the guitar while Lolly would throw words and melodies up against the wall just to see what would stick. However, my first language, musically speaking that is, would have to be the keyboard, and Lolly especially loved when I married his brilliant lyrics with the thick, rich, soulful chords that only a piano can play.

Unfortunately, unlike a guitar, these delicately-tuned

instruments cannot be patched up with a new set of strings or an adjustment to the fretboard, and my piano had certainly seen better days and better notes. I began to play my keyboard less and less when working with Lolly. I was embarrassed. I figured if I was cringing at the sour tone caused by wear and tear, a musical genius like Lolly would be tortured by it. Either his manners were very good, or his hearing was very bad.

Either way, he never said a word. That was Lolly.

Lolly was a very complex guy. He would spend an hour showing me the placement of one chord configuration, then throw a mustard jar across the room if it took more than five seconds to remove the lid. Lolly could see through bullshit the way Superman could see through drywall.

The funny thing is, most people thought Lolly lived in a perpetual state of, well, let's say, "party mode." And maybe he did, but make no mistake... Lolly Vegas *always* knew what was up, when it was up, and why it was up. And nothing proved that point more than what happened after a trip we took to the Guitar Center.

Lolly used to love to go to music stores. He rarely bought anything—maybe some sheet music or an occasional capo. Fans and fellow musicians took care of everything else, sending him guitars and percussion instruments from all over the world. Lolly was regaling the manager with stories from Redbone's glory days. Stories the manager had heard a thousand times, and to be honest, stories I had heard a million times, so I very discreetly made my way to the keyboard room. I sat behind what would be considered the iPhone 20 of pianos, as compared to mine, which would be considered a rotary dial phone. I began to play.

What did I play? "Come and Get Your Love," of course! Hey, when in Rome...

The majestic sound that emanated from this magnificent keyboard was like something out of a dream. I wanted to laugh and cry at the same time. But before I could do either, the manager interrupted me before I got to the chorus to tell me that Lolly said to meet him at the car. I left immediately. We grabbed a quick bite and headed home.

I didn't see Lolly the next day; he said he had to take care of some business. He did, however, call me at 3:00am the next night, something he was prone to doing on a regular basis. He told me he was craving deli and to bring over a pastrami sandwich sometime after noon, when he was up.

Of course, that call could have waited until the morning, when I was up. The deli was at our corner so I certainly didn't have to set sail to go there, but that was Lolly. I got to his place at 12:00noon on the dot with a pastrami sandwich on rye, coleslaw and extra pickles, just the way he liked it.

He was sitting in his favorite recliner, a beat-up family relic that even Goodwill would never take. He was watching the news. In the center of his living room stood a mammoth box with the word YAMAHA written vertically on the side.

It was *the* piano, my iPhone 20 piano that I had salivated over two days earlier.

I looked at Lolly in awe, disbelief, and I was filled with a gratitude that came up from the bowels of my being. Lolly removed his glasses, looked at me, and said (and I quote):

"Wipe that pussy look off your face, and give me my sandwich."

I just stood there stunned, and then he said, "Come on, brother, that piece of shit you were playing was getting on my nerves!" I placed the sandwich on the counter, knelt down, and wrapped my arms around him. As I held him close he whispered...

"And take that big fucking box over to your place, it's

blocking the TV."

Then he offered me half of his sandwich.

But as I keep telling you... that was Lolly.

FOR THE LOVE OF LOLLY

PARKING WARS

What is it with testosterone and parking spaces?

The anger, outrage, and thirst for blood that comes to bear when middle-aged men fight over a coveted parking spot makes *Game of Thrones* look like *When Harry Met Sally*.

Such was the case when Lolly and I pulled over one day to lunch at KFC.

Lolly and I had been working in the studio since the break of dawn. I never understood why a guy who watched *The Honeymooners* reruns until 4:00am with a Slim Jim in one hand and a bottle of Jim Beam in the other would book a recording studio before the cock crowed!

Me, I drink Yoo-Hoo and eat salads. I go to bed after the 10:00pm news.

I had to drag my ass out of bed and when I got to Lolly's, he stood at the front door. He was dressed in a red velvet jacket, wearing his signature hat with a feather from his native tribe affixed to it, singing "Spinning Wheel" by Blood Sweat and Tears at the top of his lungs.

He was either a morning person or Jim Beam had not left the building. Anyway, back to lunch....

Now, this particular Kentucky Fried Chicken was in a strip mall the size of a football field. It was noon, and it seemed like all of Los Angeles had a hankering for the Extra Crispy that day, because there wasn't a parking spot anywhere to be found.

I suggested we go somewhere else, anywhere else. (This is LA—there's an eatery on every corner!) But Lolly was craving those hockey pucks the Colonel passed off as biscuits.

I had to circle the lot so many times that I was tempted to have Lolly run into the adjoining Rite Aid to get me some Dramamine for motion sickness.

Then, out of the corner of my eye, I saw those beautiful white lights that come on when someone is backing out of a space.

I headed straight for it. Lolly was oblivious; he was harmonizing with an Air Supply song that was playing on the radio.

From the opposite direction, I saw a car headed for the space. I put on my turn signal, and so did the driver in the oncoming car. We both continued toward the spot.

It was like gunfight at the OKFC corral!

We were literally playing chicken—for chicken.

I got there first. I started to turn in but the other car obnoxiously blocked my way.

Lolly stopped singing. I begged Lolly not to get out of the car.

Lolly got out of the car.

So now I had to get out of the car.

From the other vehicle, two menacing biker-looking dudes in their mid-fifties emerged. One wore a cut-off jeans vest that exposed tattoos with a XXX rating, and the other guy was sporting a white ZZ Top beard and a leather jacket straight out of a Marlon Brando movie.

Of course I looked over at Lolly and said what any

normal person would say in this situation: "OH SHIT!"

The good ol' boys looked Lolly over and started laughing. Not funny, "ha ha" laughing, but like Charlie Manson on crack laughing.

Did I mention that Lolly was wearing a red velvet jacket with a hat and a feather?

The guy with the beard eyed Lolly up and down and then he spoke. "Hey Injun Joe, tell your boyfriend to move his car." Lolly informed him that he was straight as an arrow (if you'll pardon the pun), and if he didn't believe him, he should get his buddy's mother to vouch for it.

The other guy with the tats had veins popping out of his neck as he approached Lolly, who was loving all of this, by the way.

Me, well, my life was actually passing before my eyes.

I positioned myself in between them, hoping no one could hear my knees knocking, and I very calmly said, "I will be happy to move my car."

Now, usually I fear nothing and no one, but I am not stupid and I could see that these guys could snap Lolly and me in half like twigs. So I started to pray... "Please God, don't let Lolly say anything, please, please God, don't let Lolly say anything..."

Lolly said something, and this is what Lolly said...

"Hey fucknuts, we ain't moving our car, you and your *Deliverance*-looking, cocksucker buddy need to move your car."

Okay, so God was obviously busy at that particular moment, so I stepped in.

"Hey fellas..." (Now, I don't usually pull out the Redbone card, but quite frankly, I wanted to live.)

"Fellas, do you not know who this is?"

Mr. Tattoo: "Nah, I don't know who he is. I know *what* he

is... a dead motherfucker."

Me: "No, no, this is Lolly Vegas, the lead singer from Redbone. Guys, he had the number one song in the country, remember "Come and Get Your Love?!" I nervously started to sing, "Heeeeeyyy, Heeeeeyyy, Come and get your..."

Lolly flashed me a look that felt like he flung a ninja flying star into my esophagus... I stopped singing.

Mr. ZZ Top: "Yeah, right, how 'bout come and get your ass kicked?"

Lolly stood there, defiant, in that Superman pose that George Reeves used to do in the show's intro.

Then, Redneck Number One leaned over to Redneck Number Two and ended this confrontation the way it began, by saying "OH SHIT!"

He recognized Lolly from album covers (that he probably stored at a shack in the woods where he brought the bodies of the people he murdered). He walked over and extended a ten-point bro handshake, which of course Lolly knew (because Lolly knew everything).

At that precise moment, another parking spot opened up. Lolly invited them to grab a bite with us, on him, and the guys were honored.

As we walked up to KFC, Lolly apologized for what he said. But, it was a Lolly apology, which went like this:

"Hey dude, I didn't mean what I said about your mom. I was wrong."

The guys patted Lolly on the shoulder as I held the door open and exhaled. Then Lolly took a beat and said:

"'Cause now that I think about it, it wasn't your mom... It was your sister."

Time stood still, and then they all cracked up.

Lesson for the day... "Finger-lickin' trumps ass-kickin'!"

FOR THE LOVE OF LOLLY

AFTER THE STROKE STRUCK

Lolly had lived ten lifetimes on the road and given in to all the clichéd temptations the rock star lifestyle affords. But he always remained sharp as a tack, and possessed a mastery of the guitar that few will ever know.

This is a fact that I can surely attest to, because I have played the guitar my whole life, and to be frank, I'm pretty damn good!

But, to Lolly, his guitar was so much more than an instrument.

It had been a vehicle for his faith and his feelings, his angst and his ancestry... it was a depository for every life experience he wished to share with his audience and translate them through music.

Now when it comes to the guitar, I know every major, minor, sharp, and flat on the fretboard, but Mr. Vegas, well... he played in the key of Lolly.

Lolly was generous in spirit, heart, and talent, and there were many all-night jam sessions in his apartment where Lolly schooled me on his unique sound that can't be found on any chord chart.

When Lolly had his stroke, a few years before I met him, his world was turned upside down. He was no longer able to do the simplest of things. Tying his shoes became tantamount to climbing Mount Everest. Once I moved in, met Lolly, and became close to him, I thanked God that I lived next door to my dear friend and was able to be there for him every step of the way, to ease any frustration in not being able to do the millions of tiny tasks we all take for granted. I've got to hand it to Lolly, though, he was always cool. A quiet calm lived inside of him.

Despite the stroke and all the carnage it left in its wake, Lolly always projected a sort of Zen-like quality. A oneness with everyone and everything, even the devastating illness that fought to erase him. But Lolly would not be erased. He would find a way to outsmart this life-threatening opponent that wished to put an end to Lolly's talent. And with each day, Lolly mustered the strength and the determination to hold a guitar pick, and even manage to strum.

Forming a chord remained impossible, but Lolly had taught me so much and with his insight and brilliance, he guided me to form the chords across the guitar's neck as Lolly brought the instrument and himself back to life.

I felt so blessed, for not only was I privileged to be Lolly's right-hand man, but when he played his guitar, I was also his left-hand man!

PHOTO INTERMISSION

"Cane" & Disabled

One of Lolly's most prized possessions was an ancestral walking stick. This Native American artifact was a symbol of power and strength, and he displayed it proudly in his home. Sadly, after his stroke, the walking stick was replaced with a generic cane. I knew Lolly felt embarrassed and self-conscious having to lean, literally and figuratively, on this cheap aluminum crutch.

On his birthday, I brought over a cake and replaced that cane with a more stylish one, a sort of scepter that fit Lolly's flamboyant personality. His eyes welled up with tears of joy as I reminded him, "You have a gold record and a platinum heart… a tin cane can never change that!

Lolly always got such a big kick out of my horror & sci-fi collection.
So, one day I gifted him with a very rare piece that he had admired.
As I rolled the frightening figure into Lolly's apartment, he rose from his chair.
I was prepared for a big hug, but he walked past me and grabbed an
ornate Native American headdress that hung on his wall.
He placed it on the Mad Scientist statue.
Kind of stunned, I asked why he did that?
Lolly's reply...
"Cuz ya never see an Indian in a fucking horror film!"

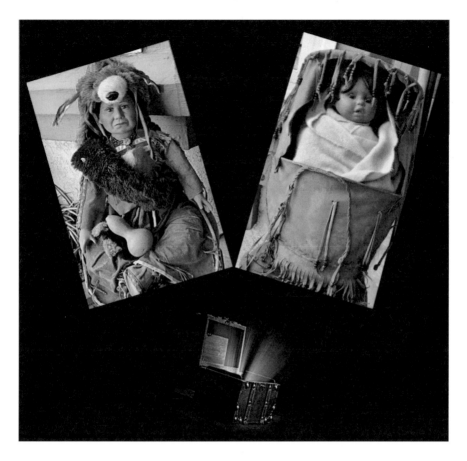

I got a call from Lolly in the middle of the night; nothing new there. He asked me to come over, and said it was important. I threw on a robe and staggered next door, half asleep. Lolly's door was unlocked, again, nothing new there. I walked in to find Lolly sitting on his chair in his pajamas.

On the sofa sat two Native American dolls. One was a baby in a papoose, the larger one seemed to be an Indian chief. Lolly said a fan had sent them and he wanted me to have them. The hour was a bit odd for gift giving, but I was touched by his generosity. I scooped up the dolls and walked Lolly back to his room. As Lolly pulled the blanket up to his chin, he thanked me for taking the dolls and told me they scared the crap out of him. I asked him "In what way?" and here's what he said...

"I saw the little fucker blink her eyes, and I think the big fucker told her to do it!"

(Now, I am not superstitious, but I keep both dolls in a locked trunk... just in case!)

LITTLE TREE, BIG HONOR

Lolly Vegas was a proud Native American, with roots in the Yaqui and Shoshone tribes. One is born into a tribe. You don't pledge it like a fraternity, or marry into it, or beg, borrow, or steal into a tribe. Native Americans take the pureness of their blood and the piety of their heritage very seriously.

Being an Italian American, I can understand this clannish attitude. One of the best examples comes from the iconic mobster movie *Goodfellas,* for though the most loyal and biggest money-maker for the "family" was the character played by Robert De Niro, because he was only half Italian, he could never be a "made" man. Again, with the blood — that's how it works.

And that is why the event I am about to share truly blew my mind.

It was a Saturday evening that seemed no different than any other, until Lolly called. He asked me to come over.

Lolly and I pretty much had a routine. You know, set times when I brought over breakfast, took him to lunch, ordered in dinner, and in the wee small hours of the morning, listened to him bitch about broads, band members, and business managers. Well, we had already shared all three daily meals and it was much too early for the bitch fest, but when Lolly called, I responded. That's what best friends do.

As I have stated earlier, Lolly had a habit of leaving his front door open, though I begged him to close it and lock it on an hourly basis. He feared nothing; he almost hoped an intruder would darken his doorstep. He believed the spirits of his ancient ancestors would scare off the would-be assailant and if that didn't work, Lolly would grab his tribal dagger from his end table and "Cut his balls off." (Lolly's expression, not mine.)

So, every time I approached his threshold I would call out his name so he knew it was me, because truth be told, I am very fond of my balls.

This time the door was only slightly ajar. After I heard Lolly yell out, "Come in ya crazy bastard" (one of Lolly's lovely nicknames for me), I pushed the door open all the way and walked in.

My eyes were assaulted by a plume of smoke and an aroma that quickly caught in my throat as I started to choke. Eyes tearing up through the fog, I could see Lolly sitting on his recliner, smiling.

"Lolly, what the hell is that smell, man?" As I stepped toward him, I heard the door close behind me. A gentleman in Native American attire walked from behind the door waving some kind of smoking plant and began to encircle me.

Lolly, half-looking at me and half-glancing at a rerun of *Good Times*, said, "That's sage, brother. That's to ward off any evil entities."

Now, as I have mentioned, I am Italian. I know basil, I know oregano, and I know parsley. Sage, I don't know.

I started to walk towards Lolly's chair, as this comrade of

his continued to circle me with the smoke from the demon-deterring sage.

"Ok pal, whatever you say. Are we worried about evil entities today?" I was placating my friend because, to be honest, I was positive he was stoned out of his mind and I was guessing that the gentleman with the sage was his pot dealer.

As I started to take my familiar seat on the sofa next to Lolly's chair, several people began to emerge from Lolly's bedroom. They, too, were attired in Native American garb. They carried feathered canes and wore animal-adorned headdresses. I was beginning to wonder if I was getting a buzz off the sage.

Lolly stood, so I stood. Lolly removed his glasses and placed his hand on my shoulder and said, "Stephen, a brother is a man that you can turn to, that you can confide in, that you can count on.

"A brother does not run away during dark times, a brother runs toward you in dark times. A brother keeps your secrets, overlooks your faults and always finds the good in you, even on the days you are no good.

"Steve, you are my brother; our bond transcends ancestry, heritage, and blood. Today I will make it official, today you become an honorary tribe member."

That's when I realized the guy with the sage was not a dealer—he was the real deal!

Eyes tearing up, this time from sentiment and not the sage, I hugged Lolly and told him my heart was full and I would be so proud to be a part of his magnificent tribe.

Lolly christened me "Little Tree."

Being the gavone that I am, I was hoping for a more forceful name, like "Big Tree," "Powerful Tree," "Don't Fuck with Me Tree..."

But then, Lolly went on to explain that a "Little Tree" continues to grow, with its branches always moving closer to the heavens.

I was humbled by this reverent moment, though it was a bit hard to keep a straight face while J.J. Evans yelled out "Dynomite!" in the background.

Lolly had not turned off the TV during the sacred ceremony, and since he was a bit hard of hearing from years of rock music, the volume was on 11!

Then Lolly sat me down. When he took his seat on the recliner, the other members of the tribe took their seats on the floor. (I instinctively reached for the television clicker and hit "mute.")

Lolly told me that I must always uphold the philosophy of his people—that I must make my decisions with great care, that now I was part of something much bigger than myself.

He then began to regale us with an ancestral story, surrounded by his fellow tribesmen, which now included me.

Lolly spoke of an ancient elder chief whose time had come to inject wisdom and warning into the heart of his grandson who was on the cusp of becoming a man, and would soon marry and head into battle. The chief spoke of two wolves engaged in a standoff.

One wolf was kind, and fair, and believed in himself and the goodness of people. The other wolf was angry, vengeful, full of self-doubt, and skeptical of everything and everyone. He explained that this is the struggle that lives inside all of us. These two wolves will stand at the crossroads and will not rest until one is defeated.

The Chief's grandson asked, "Which one will live?"

The Chief placed his hand against the young man's heart

and said, "The one that you feed."

This story resonated so much for me, for I was certainly guilty of feeding the wrong wolf on many occasions.

I began to see things in a much different light. I began to weigh decisions with a whole new insight. That was a gift of a lifetime that Lolly bestowed upon me.

My dear friend honored me with another gift that day. Lolly always carried a suede shoulder bag. He threw everything in it, and never left the house without it. It was crafted by Native Americans and was one of his most prized possessions. Yeah, I guess it was a purse, but on Lolly it looked totally badass.

The day I became "one of his people," Lolly presented me with an exact replica of his precious bag. He had it made especially for me, especially for this sacred occasion. I'm pretty sure that when I carry the bag, this "Little Tree" does not look as badass as Lolly, but then again, nobody could.

And that's how I became an honorary tribesman.

My story might sound a little "CRAZY" (Horse)…

But that's how it happened… and that's no (Sitting) "BULL!"

"GLOCK" AND ROLL HOOCHIE KOO

We all remember this famous line from the film *Forrest Gump*: "Life is like a box of chocolates, you never know what you're going to get." Well, with Mr. Vegas, "Life is like a box of dynamite, and what you're going to get is... BLOWN UP!"

There are so many examples of this, it's hard to know where to start, but let's go with a "Life with Lolly" situation that nearly got me five to ten in San Quentin!

It started off as a normal movie night at Lolly's. Now, quite frankly, for Lolly, money was no object. He could have wined and dined at every famed eatery in Hollywood, every night of the week, for the rest of his life. But that wasn't Lolly. He preferred to spend his nights in his modest Encino apartment with a leftover Carl's Junior hamburger, a near beer, and his neighbor and best pal, a.k.a me, by his side.

Lolly was not childish by any means; in fact, he was one of the savviest people I have ever met. But he was child-like. He took such pleasure and delight in simple things. He would sit and watch reruns of *I Love Lucy*, *The Honeymooners*, *Good Times*, and laugh out loud, even though he had seen the episodes dozens of times. I had more fun watching Lolly's joyful reaction to these classic shows than watching the shows themselves, and it was a sitcom-binging night like that where my story begins.

Lolly always sat on his throne. His musical prowess had earned him a throne of gold encrusted with precious gems, but Lolly being Lolly, he preferred a beat-up, faux leather Barcalounger. Now in all fairness, it was a reclining chair, but that function had ceased to work many reruns ago. I used to sit on the equally dilapidated sofa. The great irony was that Lolly kept boxes of priceless artifacts on this couch: gold records, numerous awards, tribal relics, photos with everyone from Stevie Wonder to Stevie Nicks, all on this crappy piece of furniture that Sanford and Son would have left at the curbside. There was room for only one person to sit, and it was a tight squeeze at that.

So this one night Lolly and I were watching a *Gomer Pyle* marathon. Lolly got an especially big kick out of Jim Nabors playing a shy hick from the sticks with a singing voice that could shake the rafters. As I was watching, it occurred to me that I hadn't heard Lolly laugh at the spots where he always laughed, which I knew by heart because we had seen this particular episode a thousand times. I turned to look at him and was taken aback to see Lolly frozen in his seat like a stone statue.

His eyes were glazed over and the only sign of life was the sound of aluminum crinkling as his hand involuntarily crushed his beer can in slow motion.

I yelled out his name and began to gently shake him. He was not in there and fear gripped me like a vise.

I called 911 and the ambulance came within five of the most terrifying minutes I have ever experienced. In Los Angeles, as well as many other places I suppose, several police officers accompany the rescue squad to the call. When they all arrived, Lolly tried to speak but nothing came out.

The paramedics examined him and diagnosed that he was

having a series of mini-seizures. They loaded him onto a gurney as the two uniformed police officers walked around the room eyeing the framed album covers that hung on the walls. I could tell that they were beginning to realize that this was no ordinary call and that this body was "somebody."

One cop asked what my relationship was to Lolly and asked that I produce some ID. I whipped out my driver's license and the cop handed it back with a nod. The other cop then asked for Lolly's ID to bring to the hospital.

Lolly was wearing sweat pants with no pockets, so it was obvious that his wallet was not in his pants. I looked on the coffee table, kitchen counter, night table, bathroom sink, between the sofa cushions... I even forcibly reclined the recliner and pressed my hand into the void where Jimmy Hoffa's body might have been discovered, but no wallet.

The paramedic informed me that it was imperative for insurance reasons and medical history. Personally, I think he wanted to see if this disheveled, lovable rocker had any priors. Then one of the officers said "Check in there," and motioned to the large armoire against the wall. It was a family heirloom made of sumptuous mahogany with carved bison and palomino horses that adorned the doors and sported gilded bronze hardware (and yes, I knew all this because Lolly and I also watched *Antiques Roadshow*).

Anyway, though I had always admired the outside, I had never peeked inside. At the officer's cordial yet firm request, I pulled the double doors apart, which revealed a wall of drawers. As I opened the first drawer, I did not find Lolly's wallet.

What I *did* find was Lolly's stash. Rows of zip-locked bags of weed, enough to make Cheech and Chong blush. I inadvertently slammed the drawer shut.

The cops who were gathering Lolly's shoes and turning off the TV glanced over at me.

I gave them a frozen smile then proceeded to open the second drawer. More bags of marijuana, this time with pipes, and rolling papers, and bongs. (Oh my!)

I could feel the officer standing behind me as he asked "Any luck?" I replied "No," too petrified to open the third drawer. The officer's radio went off, and he walked toward the front door, perhaps to get better reception.

I slowly slid open drawer number three praying, "Don't let it be more pot, don't let it be more pot..."

It was not more pot. It was a Glock semi-automatic pistol with a dozen cartridges lined up next to it.

I slowly and silently closed the drawer. I could feel the beads of sweat dripping from my temple into my ears. The officer on the radio walked over in a hurry.

"We've got another call, ya need a hand with that, pal?"

At that moment I pictured Lolly and I watching *Green Acres* in a common area of prison wearing matching orange jumpsuits.

Right then, Lolly lifted his head and pointed toward his half-eaten bacon cheeseburger sitting on the end table. I walked over, and there, being used as a coaster, was the infamous wallet—the worn and torn brown leather covered in ranch dressing.

I snatched it up, yelling out, "I've got it, let's go, I've got the wallet," realizing the Holy Spirit had intervened through Lolly and saved my sorry ass from an aiding and abetting charge.

The paramedics guided Lolly out the front door. As the last set of wheels rolled over the threshold, Lolly once again lifted his head, and this time, motioned toward the armoire.

And then, he spoke...

His words were garbled, but when they left his lips the gurney came to a screeching halt. The officer, following up the rear, slowly turned toward me the way Lieutenant Columbo would slowly turn to the cringing criminal in the last five minutes of the episode.

The cop asked me, "What did he say?"

Re-enter the Holy Spirit:

"He said 'Lock up the door, with my key!'"

The cop nodded, and I nearly passed out, because I understood Lolly perfectly... and what he *actually* said was:

"Glock's in the drawer, with my weed!"

The police took off, and I was still a free man!

I met Lolly at the hospital, and thank goodness he was treated and released with medication.

To this day I can't hear the *Gomer Pyle* theme without peeing in my pants a little. But in Lolly's world, it was just an ordinary Tuesday night.

DUMB & DUMBER

Here is a multiple choice question for all of Lolly's fans and my devoted readers.

This is a photo of:

    A. Friends sharing a joyous occasion

    B. Pals celebrating a birthday

    C. Amigos smiling for the camera

Have you locked in your answers?

Well, sadly, none of you got it right, because the answer is...

D. As in Dumbbells, Dopes, and Doofuses courting DEATH!

Most people would think they were looking at one man holding a cigarette and another holding a cake, but the truth is, we are both holding .357 Magnums.

Lolly's went off and killed him.

Mine went off, but for the grace of God, the bullet found an exit wound.

Let's start with Lolly's weapon of choice: Marlboros.

He smoked all his life. As a teenager, as a struggling musician, and as a successful, road-weary rock-and-roll warrior. As I have stated many times in this collection of remembrances, Lolly was not a stupid man. In fact, he was one of the most educated people I have ever known. When it came to health and the effects of smoking on the body, he was book smart, Internet smart, and most importantly, due to his Native American heritage, "medicine man smart!"

Add all those smarts up and it equaled... Lolly didn't give a shit!

Lolly liked to smoke, Lolly liked to drink, Lolly liked women, and Lolly liked to rock and roll. I guess any of those things could have killed him, but the winner was the Marlboros.

I loved Lolly like my own flesh and blood, and Lolly felt the same about me. There was nothing that Lolly wouldn't do for me, or *didn't* do for me. But the smoking, well, that was Lolly's Apple Tree in his Garden of Eden.

Any favor, wish, or request was mine for the asking in that garden, but I had to lay off that proverbial Apple Tree, which was my undying beseeching for Lolly to quit. I believe the smoking affected Lolly's beautiful voice, his breathing, his taste buds, his skin, his heart, and it contributed to his stroke and eventually ended this beautiful man's life, and there wasn't a damn thing I could do about it.

Now, let's talk about yours truly.

Well, I didn't have one-tenth of Lolly's smarts. But I had the same temptations, for I, too, was a teenager, struggling musician, and was blessed to become a road-weary rock-and-roll warrior. A cigarette never touched my lips. Neither did coffee, drugs, or alcohol. But what did touch my lips was food.

That was my weapon of choice. That's how I filled the void, soothed the pain, and comforted my many heartaches. I drowned myself in White Castle hamburgers when I lost my parents. I buried myself with Popeye's chicken when a job fell through. I barricaded myself in with Taco Bell Grande Nachos when a girl broke my heart.

My drug dealers were Drake's Cakes, Little Debbie, and Hostess. And when Lolly left my life, that was a great excuse to gorge on anything I could get my hands on. Ironically, the food did not make me fat, which believe it or not, turned out to be a very bad thing. Had I become grossly overweight, I would have stopped.

I had to go on stage most nights, and I don't think my band mates would have appreciated me trading my spandex for sweats.

No, the food affected me in a much more deadly way. It predisposed me for Type II diabetes, put my blood pressure through the roof, and put a gigantic strain on my heart.

The cigarettes killed Lolly.

The food took aim, took the shot, and the Burger King bullet exited my body, for with the love and help of my friends and family, I have embraced a healthier lifestyle. I'll be honest with you, there is no way a carrot can replace a calzone, but at least I can reach the top of the stairs without gasping for breath.

I wish my dearest compadre Lolly could have joined me on my new-found journey towards health, but Lolly lived his life his way and you've got to respect that.

So yeah, when I look at this photo of us clutching those time bombs, the only word that comes to mind is "Bang!"

Yet somehow, I was spared. I was able to find a foxhole to take cover in, and I find peace in knowing that's exactly the way Mr. Vegas would have wanted it.

GOING, GOING, GONE

The last few months I had with Lolly were both enlightening and excruciating. Lolly was one of the most no-nonsense people I have ever known. He knew that his body had purchased a one-way ticket on the "I'm outta here" train, and he accepted it.

In all fairness, he had gotten his money's worth out of it by way of wine, women, and song. Still, there was so much more living to be done by this man who truly knew how to squeeze every drop out of life. But like everything in this world that has an expiration date, Lolly's came, and though it was not unexpected, the kick in the gut that his passing left behind was no less potent.

For me, Lolly's last day on this earth began the way most days did. I got up, walked my beloved dogs, and went to visit Lolly in his new home, which was one town over from me. I did this a couple of times a day. I really can't tell you if it was more for Lolly or for me, I just enjoyed his company so much. No matter how poorly he was feeling, he never failed to make me laugh, and his perpetual fountain of wisdom shaped my life in so many ways.

I never entered Lolly's dwelling without something to eat in hand. Now let's face it, Lolly had money. The guy was the founding member of one of the most popular and successful bands both nationally and globally. His hit single "Come and Get Your Love" was not only a super hit record, but has been featured in countless commercials and blockbuster movies.

When it came to his cuisine, Lolly could have had lobsters flown in from Maine or Kobe steaks flown in from Japan, but Lolly was a junk food junkie. He preferred Carl's Junior to chateaubriand, and Popeye's to poached oysters. On that last day, I brought him an Egg McMuffin and hash browns.

The food never left the bag.

As I pulled into the circular driveway I saw a car that I recognized as his brother's. My heart leapt from my chest to my throat. The front door was ajar and Lolly's brother motioned for me to come in.

I walked straight to Lolly's room. He was almost unrecognizable. I had just seen him the evening before, yet somehow the precursor to death had moved in overnight and made itself at home. I sat at his bedside. I made feeble attempts at jokes, and Lolly managed a weak smile, more for my benefit than as a result of my wit. I tried so hard to hide the fear in my eyes, I couldn't.

After a while, he fell asleep. I whispered that I would be back in a couple of hours. I chatted with more family members who had arrived, and then headed back home.

As I walked in the door I saw my answering machine flashing. Now usually this makes me very happy; it could be a booking for a gig, or news that one of my rare collectibles had been shipped, or the gorgeous blonde I met at the farmer's market returning my call... but I instinctively knew it was none of those things. It was a message that Lolly was gone, and as the words sunk in, my heart dropped from my throat to the bottom of my stomach.

I gave the family their privacy but returned the next morning to extend my condolences and to see for myself that my friend was really gone. I knocked on the door and Lolly's estranged wife Risa slowly opened the door. She and Lolly had not been together for many years, but Lolly had made a promise that he would always take care of her, and he always did.

She welcomed me with a warm embrace. She told me that she knew more than anyone how much I meant to Lolly. It was so odd to hear it put that way, because in my mind, it was always about how much Lolly meant to *me*. I walked into his room. I knew he wouldn't be in there, but I was stunned to see the medical supply place had already repo'ed the hospital bed.

I felt sick. I felt lost.

Risa was folding some of Lolly's clothes. She told me to take something, anything, as a memento. I looked around the living room, which resembled the rock and roll hall of fame.

I couldn't take a framed gold record. After all, it wasn't my song; it wasn't my achievement. I couldn't take one of his many guitars—his fingers had created the magic on them, not mine. I couldn't take any of his Native American artifacts, for although I was made an honorary member of the tribe, without Lolly as my "godfather" who grandfathered me in, I felt I could no longer lay claim to his heritage.

She offered me a pair of his athletic shoes. Lolly was a sneaker nut! His collection was sublime: leather, suede, canvas, hand-painted, bedazzled, bejeweled, and purchased from every corner of the world. But I could not get myself to pick out a pair, for though we wore the same size, I knew I could never fill his shoes. I politely declined her generous offer, and as I hugged her goodbye, I caught sight of a crumpled-up Chinese takeout menu on the end table. It was stained with soy sauce and had a ring from the near beer Lolly had placed on it like a coaster.

I was instantly transported back to the days when Lolly's body started to shut down and I could no longer entice him with any of his favorite fast foods. He was gaunt and so thin and weak. I drove to a Walgreens to get him some chocolate-flavored Boost, as prescribed by his doctor. He wouldn't touch the vanilla, and I knew he wouldn't drink the chocolate either, but I had to try something, anything.

As I sat impatiently waiting for the traffic light to turn green, I noticed Lolly's favorite Chinese restaurant on the corner. I turned in and ordered Kung Pao chicken and egg drop soup. What the hell did I have to lose?

Lolly loved it! He ate it all and sent me back for more the next day. Then he tried the shrimp with lobster sauce and beef with broccoli, the spare ribs and won ton soup. He was getting some of his strength back and he was eating with gusto without being begged and he was enjoying it. My heart soared.

Then with a crash I came back down to reality, to the world without Lolly. I told Risa I wanted the menu. She looked at me like I was nuts. She said it was garbage, but she was wrong... to me it was priceless. And best of all, it was my accomplishment!

MOVING, LITERALLY & FIGURATIVELY

I moved out of my Encino apartment a few months after Lolly died. Too many memories, too sad, too hard to walk past his front door every day knowing he was no longer behind it. He'd no longer be blasting his stereo well into the evening with the belief that neighbors around the courtyard were enjoying the free entertainment. Sometimes, depending on his back-up singers Jim Beam, Johnny Walker, and Jose Cuervo, those concerts started after midnight.

The silence was now deafening.

Not long after his passing, new tenants rented Lolly's place. I was walking up the path to my apartment and saw a woman pushing an elderly gentleman in a wheelchair. I reluctantly introduced myself to my new neighbor and she introduced herself, and then introduced the man in the chair as her father.

I went to shake his hand, but he was unresponsive, he was somewhere lost inside himself. There was a set of a few stairs that led up to Lolly's old apartment, and unfortunately the gentleman's daughter had not planned for this. However, I offered to help and picked up the back of the wheelchair while she steadied the front, and lifted it the few feet to place the gentleman on the landing in front of her door.

I then held the door open as she rolled her father into the living room, and I couldn't help but notice the bare, freshly painted walls. Walls where Lolly Vegas's gold records, framed album covers, photos with famed musicians, and priceless guitars once hung.

I felt enraged and cheated, and also hurt with an overwhelming sense of great karmic unfairness. Melodic brilliance and beauty recently occupied this sacred space, and now a new tenant with no connection to himself, let alone the legacy of Redbone's rhythmic royalty, would ever know the sanctity of the rooms in which he now resided.

My heart was in my throat as tears filled my eyes, but then I noticed an open box on the sofa. It was filled with framed military medals, an American flag, and photos of a handsome and vibrant young man in uniform that I could only assume was this withering, poor soul before me who was barely able to make eye contact.

I knew that this man's memorabilia and contribution to this world would now hang on those walls.

I walked back to my apartment realizing that Lolly also served his country. His music brought so much joy and love; his songs formed so many memories for so many people. I was sure that many young soldiers listened to Lolly's songs back in the day, and perhaps it gave them a tiny respite from the horrors they faced.

Lolly would have loved that his walls were re-covered with mementos of this man's pride and passion. A man who had once been energetic and full of life, just like Lolly, but was reduced to a man whose body no longer wished to cooperate... just like Lolly.

I felt a sense of calm, but that feeling was short-lived, for my new neighbor died a month later.

I moved a week after that, and have never returned to the San Fernando Valley. But from time to time, I can't help but wonder what hangs on those walls today.

Forever my brother...
Rest In Peace

Lolly & Stephen

FOR THE LIFE OF LOLLY

By now, you all know that Lolly is gone.

I had to put off writing this final chapter (of the final chapter) until the end of the book.

Had I relived it sooner, I might have scrapped the whole thing, and deprived his fans of the wild and woolly, lovely and loony life he led.

So let us now go to the chapel.

It was standing room only, just like one of his concerts. (Lolly would have loved that.)

The crowd was a mix of friends, family, fans, and the famous. Members of his tribe stood solemn and serene, like guardians at the gate.

The celebrant of the service was the Reverend Della Reese.

This talented singer and actress was an ordained minister, a friend of Lolly's, and throughout the years, he frequented her church to hear her preach.

Many people who adored Lolly got to say a few words about this unique and extraordinary man. I wish I could share some of their words, which I am sure were heartfelt and comforting, but I didn't hear them.

All I could hear was the deafening internal screams in my

head that kept repeating: "This can't be real, this can't be happening..."

I had been looking down at my shoes the whole time. I didn't want to raise my eyes and see that open wooden box that was now the final resting place of my dearest pal.

I knew that I would be asked to speak. I clutched a crinkled-up piece of paper with a little speech that I had written in a feeble attempt to express my sorrow.

As I slowly lifted my eyes, I noticed the parishioners were looking back at me, which was strange. I snapped out of my bereaved trance and realized that Reverend Reese was calling me up to the altar.

My legs felt like lead and my heart even heavier. As I made my way to the front of the chapel, I caught sight of Lolly's mother, Eloise. I knew my grief was real and thick and debilitating, but I could not begin to imagine the searing pain that Lolly's mom must have felt as her eyes were transfixed on the lifeless body of her son.

Lolly had been so in tune with nature and the natural progression of things... but there is nothing natural about burying your child. It is unfortunately, and heartbreakingly, the task of the child to bury their beloved parent.

As I continued to make my way toward Lolly's mom, I was transported back to the day I lost my precious mother.

I was three thousand miles away when it happened. I received the news from my sister Lisa, who tried so hard to comfort me, but nothing could.

Since Lolly was not only my best friend, but my next-door neighbor, he was the first person I told, and when I did, he burst into tears.

"Why are YOU crying?" I asked him, and he replied...

"Because today your beautiful mother saw the face of Jesus!"

As I reached her pew, I veered to the right and took Lolly's mother in my arms. I thanked her for bringing her wonderful boy into this world—for gifting me with the best friend I had ever had. She patted me on the back and nodded her head.

She was frail and quite elderly, but she was strong and managed to stay composed as the tears silently streamed down her cheeks. She had instilled Lolly with that formidable strength and because of my deep bond with Lolly, some of that strength had rubbed off on me. I tried to keep that in mind as I took my place at the Reverend Reese's side.

I stood in front of the crowd and locked eyes with Della.

She whispered, "Go ahead. Say what you have to say, son."

Ha, easier said than done. What I wanted to say was, "WHY??"

Thank goodness I had my cheat sheet so I could quickly read it and disappear into the crowd and grieve in private.

As I held the paper in my hands, though, I realized that I had rubbed away the ink with my sweaty, nervous palms, and I could only make out a few words.

I looked out over the people who were mourning just like me, then over at Lolly whose casket adorned the sanctuary.

I started to smile, because I began to remember the time Lolly and I had dinner at this swanky hotel with a doorman.

It had been raining, which was rare in Los Angeles, and I was holding Lolly's doggie bag and umbrella in one hand, and guiding Lolly, who now walked with a cane, with the other hand.

The doorman was perched under an awning in an effort to keep dry, and made no attempt to help us. I balanced the doggie bag, umbrella, and Lolly, while fumbling for my keys and pushed the doors open with my foot.

Once out onto the street, Lolly smiled at this useless doorman and turned to me and said, "Give him a twenty."

"But Lolly, he didn't even open the door for us!"

"You're right," Lolly said. "So fuck it. Just give him ten."

That was Lolly.

I knew I couldn't share that particular story with this crowd in this sacred place, but there were so many sweet and screwball tales I *could* tell. I shoved the paper in my pocket and began to share the many moments that formed one of the greatest friendships of all time.

It was like Lolly's spirit had reached out to me, and eased my fear and fret over losing him. The whole somber mood of the room began to lighten up, and what a gift that was.

But as I stepped down, I touched the cross that was draped across Lolly's still body.

It was the cross I had given him, and a deep sadness began to overtake my heart and soul, for I knew this was the last time I would ever see my friend.

I wanted to etch his every facial feature into my brain as I started my long walk down the center aisle toward the exit.

It was like walking the last mile on death row, but instead of the electric chair, which would have been mercifully quick and final, my sentence was to be a long and painful life without my best friend.

The closer I got to the door, the harder it became to choke back the tears.

As I glanced back for one final look, an elderly woman with a kind face and soft blue eyes approached me. I didn't recognize her; I didn't know if she was a friend of Lolly's or simply a fan in mourning.

She told me that the anecdotes about Lolly that I had shared with the congregation were both heart-breaking and heart-warming.

I managed a faint smile and as I turned to leave, I felt her hand lightly graze my shoulder.

I heard her say that I needed to write down those stories, and share them with every person that Lolly Vegas had touched throughout the world...

And so I did!

Stephen Rosario Pisani

EPILOGUE

Though my time on earth with Lolly Vegas had come to an end, there was still unfinished business between us.

In his last days, Lolly's fiery presence was reduced to embers, but the flame from his brilliant creativity still burned brightly.

He began to pen what would be the final lyrics to the soundtrack of his life.

These coffee-stained words of inspiration were hand-written by Lolly, and left in my care.

I was honored when he asked me to finish his song and share it with his fans!

And so I will...

For The Love Of Lolly
(A Labor of Love)

"I want to thank the readers for taking this emotional journey with me.
Reliving and retelling the stories contained in this book
has been the hardest, yet most cathartic task I have ever taken on.
There were so many times I wanted to walk away from this project and
leave the sacred memories I shared with Lolly safe, secured and silenced.
But then you would never get to know this gentle, generous genius.
Though I can no longer pick up a phone, text or go visit Lolly Vegas,
I pray this collection of memories will inspire you to...
pick up a phone, text and go visit YOUR best pal."

Wishing you love, happiness & friendship,
Steve

ACKNOWLEDGEMENTS

My heartfelt thanks to:

My sister, Lisa Brandi, for taking my stories, memories, and photographs, and crafting them into the powerful, moving, and entertaining tales you now see before you.

My editor, Gretchen Joy, for all of her work in guiding this project to its final publication.

My friends, who always believed in me and this book:
Laura Sweeney, John Burke, Kristina McElyea, Stacy Phares, Barbara Rew, Julie Roman, Mathew Fetzer, Jodi Lowry, Ronda Arnold, Arnold and Patricia Lieberman, Mary Ann McCaffery, Geri L. Van Teslaar, Suzanne Grooms, Rolly O'Fearadhaigh, Jerri-Lynn Webb, Aaron and Michelle Calloway, Carol Espinosa, Linda Collier, Cindra Reaume-Weber, Anjelle Ebright-Harmon… and so many more; your support has meant the world to me.

My extended family, Joe Dominguez and Petra Morales, two wonderful people introduced to me by Lolly!

ABOUT STEPHEN

Stephen Rosario Pisani hails from the great state of New Jersey. Growing up in a show business family, it's only natural that Stephen would go into the family business. The musical genes come by way of his mom, Anne, the founding member of singing quintet The Five DeMarco Sisters.
(You can hear their beautiful blend on YouTube.)

His love for the stage, television, and film sets comes from the paternal side, compliments of his father, actor and director Remo Pisani.
(Watch his film and television clips on YouTube.)

When Stephen's mom remarried, she and her new husband, Jimmy Rose, made their living as a harmonizing, guitar-playing duo, and performed all over the country. (Yup, they're on YouTube too!)

Stephen has been performing since he was a child. His parents would bring him to their gig and place him between his two sisters, Lisa and Jamie, and they would sing for their supper... literally!

Stephen never met a musical instrument he didn't like. He is adept on the bass, acoustic guitar, electric guitar, grand piano, and synthesizer. As a teen he played in rock bands, metal bands, jazz bands and folk bands. He is as comfortable composing a movie score as he is writing a hard rock anthem. He has opened for Orleans, Bob Hope, Steppenwolf, America, Roy Orbison, and Bobby Rydell (to name a few). Stephen has written and produced seven albums. His latest single is entitled "Lolly's Song," a haunting ballad that he wrote as a companion piece for his memoir, *For the Love of Lolly*, and as musical tribute to his best friend Lolly Vegas.

You can listen to it here on YouTube:
https://youtu.be/wI0yyKgWZTQ/

After playing every venue in New Jersey from Newark to Neptune, Stephen felt he had to take a chance and dive into his Dad's gene pool and give acting a try.

"Said Californy is the place he oughta be, so he packed up his dog and they moved to Beverly... Hills, that is!"

Once in La La Land, Stephen got his start performing stunts and acting in countless films and television shows, including *Star Trek: Deep Space Nine*, *Star Trek: Voyager*, *Strong Medicine*, *ER*, *The Office*, *Castle*, *Without a Trace*, *Standoff*, *Delivering Milo*, *Lucky Numbers*, *Mimic 2*, and *The Fast and the Furious* (to name a few).

When Stephen was a little boy watching Chiller Theater, he was introduced to the Universal Studios horror hit parade that included Frankenstein, Count Dracula, The Mummy, The Wolfman, The Invisible Man, and The Creature From The Black Lagoon (to name a few). He was fascinated by the actors, the special effects makeup, and the stories. He never grew out of that fascination, and has befriended the mold makers and men and women behind the makeup of the most famous horror and sci-fi movies and TV shows ever made.

Stephen's collection is world-renowned and includes a replicated figure from every nightmare ever produced for the screen. Check it out on his website **FearForSale.com**... if you dare!

To listen to "Lolly's Song" and many other original compositions penned by Stephen, visit his YouTube channel or his music website:

YouTube.com/startrekstuntman
SongsByStephen.com

I GET BY WITH A LITTLE HELP FROM MY FRIENDS!

Made in United States
Troutdale, OR
04/17/2024

19183181R00052